NIGHT STALKERS

U.S. SPECIAL FORCES

NIGHT STALKERS

JIM WHITING

CREATIVE EDUCATION · CREATIVE PAPERBACKS

PUBLISHED BY Creative Education and Creative Paperbacks

P.O. Box 227, Mankato, Minnesota 56002

Creative Education and Creative Paperbacks are imprints of

The Creative Company

www.thecreativecompany.us

DESIGN BY Christine Vanderbeek; **PRODUCTION BY** Liddy Walseth

ART DIRECTION BY Rita Marshall

PRINTED IN CHINA

PHOTOGRAPHS BY

Alamy (AF archive, Rafael Ben-Ari, Everett Collection Historical,
Image Bank, Moviestore collection Ltd, PJF Military Collection,
Maurice Savage, Stocktrek Images, Inc., Tebnad, US Air Force Photo,
US Army Photo, Z2A1), DVIDS (1st Lt. Henry Chan, Cpl. Carlos Jimenez,
Sgt. Christopher Prows), iStockphoto (spxChrome), Shutterstock
(ALMAGAMI, AMFPhotography, Pavel Chagochkin, Wojtek
Chmielewski, Michael Fitzsimmons, gst, Keith Tarrier)

LIBRARY OF CONGRESS CATALOGING-IN-PUBLICATION DATA

Names: Whiting, Jim, author.

Title: Night Stalkers / Jim Whiting.

Series: U.S. Special Forces.

Includes bibliographical references and index.

Summary: A chronological account of the American military special
forces unit known as Night Stalkers, including key details about
important figures, landmark missions, and controversies.

Identifiers: LCCN 2017051386 / ISBN 978-1-60818-985-4 (hardcover) / ISBN
978-1-62832-612-3 (pbk) / ISBN 978-1-64000-086-5 (eBook)

Subjects: LCSH: 1. United States. Army. Special Operations Aviation
Regiment (Airborne), 160th—Juvenile literature. 2. Night and all-
weather operations (Military aeronautics)—United States—Juvenile
literature. 3. Military helicopters—United States—Juvenile literature.

Classification: LCC UA34.S64 W46 2018 / DDC 356/.1660973—dc23

CCSS: RI.5.1, 2, 3, 8; RH.6-8.4, 5, 6, 8

FIRST EDITION HC 9 8 7 6 5 4 3 2 1

FIRST EDITION PBK 9 8 7 6 5 4 3 2 1

U.S. SPECIAL FORCES

TABLE OF CONTENTS

★ ★ ★

Night Stalkers often rely on night-vision goggles to carry out their missions.

FORCE FACTS Night-vision goggles are an essential part of Night Stalker equipment. The German army introduced the technology in 1939, and the goggles have undergone many improvements since then.

FORCE FACTS MH stands for multi-mission helicopter, while AH means attack helicopter—one that carries weapons for mission support.

INTRODUCTION

THE DUST WAS STILL SETTLING ON THE RUINS OF NEW YORK City's World Trade Center on September 11, 2001, when American military leaders began planning a response. The target was obvious: Afghanistan. Osama bin Laden had established training camps there for the terrorists who had hijacked the planes that were flown into buildings that day.

The first step of that response involved inserting small teams of United States Army Special Forces (commonly known as Green Berets) to work with friendly Afghans. Their goal was to overthrow the ruling *Taliban*, which had helped bin Laden set up the camps. The Taliban had also killed many of their countrymen since taking control in 1996.

The Green Berets needed to be transported to Afghanistan in lumbering MH-47 Chinook helicopters at night under terrible weather conditions. The flight assignment fell to the 160th Special Operations Aviation Regiment (Airborne), or SOAR (A), better known as Night Stalkers. These soldiers depended on their training and skill to deal with sandstorms, snow, ice, rain, high winds, sudden changes in elevation, and other obstacles. "Just imagine flying when you can't see three feet (1 m) in front of you for a couple of hours, landing or hoping the weather would clear so you could refuel, and then flying through the mountains all the while getting shot at," said a flight engineer.

Even the landing was dangerous. There were no assurances that their reception would be friendly. Fortunately, the helicopters set down safely, and the Green Berets started on their mission. Within weeks, the Taliban was driven from Afghanistan.

As multi-mission helicopters, Chinooks used by the Night Stalkers are made for low-level, nighttime flight.

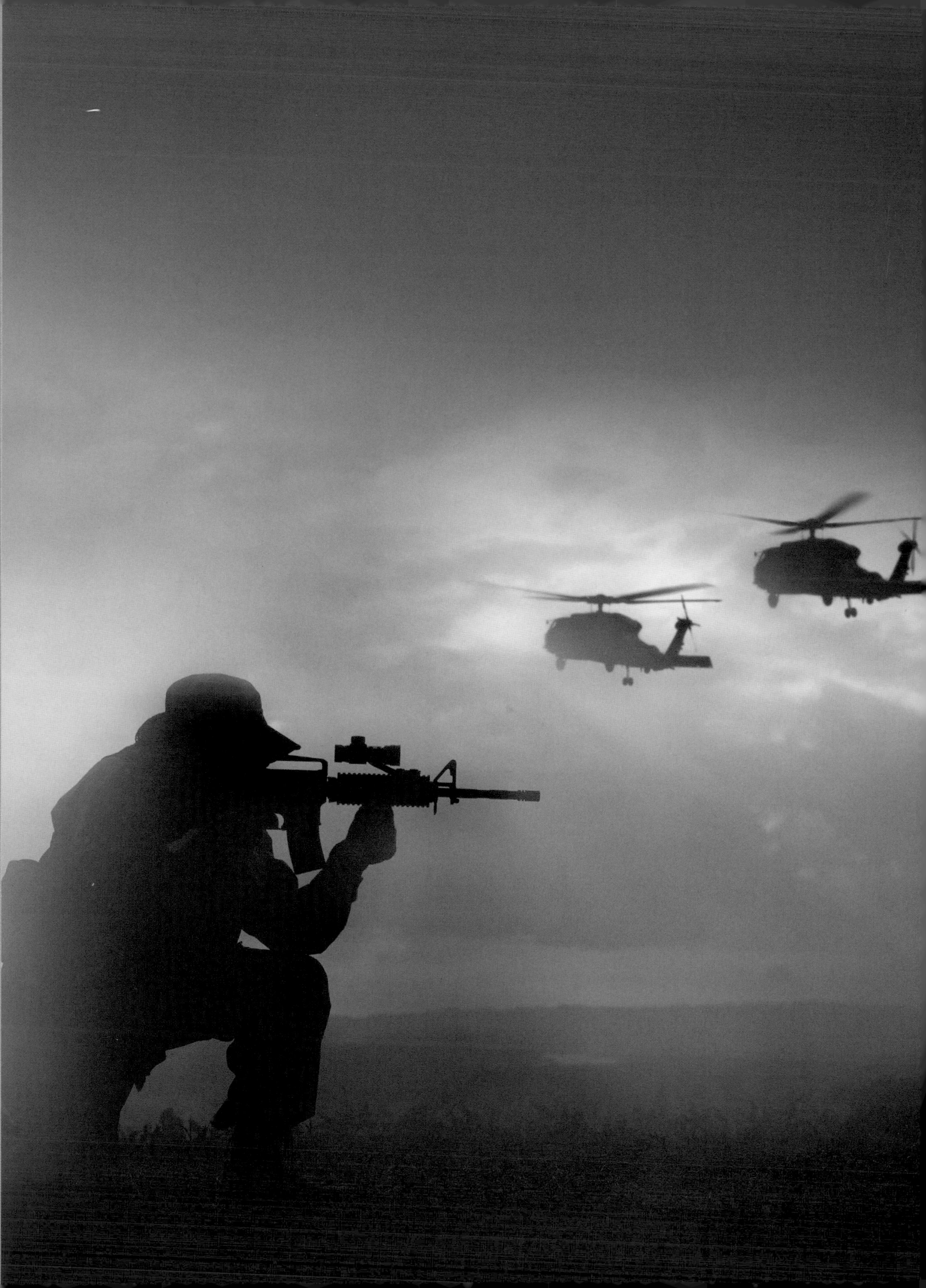

DEATH WAITS IN THE DARK

America's Special Forces are among the world's best. Years of grueling training prepare Delta Force, Green Berets, Navy SEALs, and other forces to perform at the highest level in hundreds of dangerous missions every year. These missions are almost always successful. But to carry them out, the operators have to reach the mission site. Often, they arrive by helicopter. The little-known Night Stalkers serve as the American Special Forces delivery organization. It's no accident that author Fred J. Pushies uses a variation on FedEx's 1978 tagline—"When it absolutely, positively has to be there overnight"—to describe the Night Stalkers: "In the special operations community, they are heralded as the best helicopter pilots in the world," Pushies writes. "When it absolutely, positively has to be on site, on time, in the dead of the night, plus or minus 30 seconds, the aircrews of the 160th SOAR (A) deliver."

But unlike FedEx customers, who eagerly await the arrival of a package, those on the receiving end of a Night Stalkers delivery have no desire to see them and may greet them with gunfire and other weaponry. The pilots and crew are fully aware of the dangers, but that doesn't deter them from their missions. Fittingly, "Night Stalkers Don't Quit" is one of the unit's mottoes. Because most missions take place after nightfall, another motto is "Death Waits in the Dark."

Black Hawks are used and depended upon by nearly every branch of the U.S. military.

FORCE FACTS Because of the distinctive shape of its cockpit, the Little Bird helicopter is nicknamed the "Killer Egg."

The Night Stalkers owe their existence to one of the darkest episodes in recent American history. On November 4, 1979, hundreds of young Iranians swarmed into the U.S. embassy in Tehran. In defiance of recognized international standards, they held 52 American personnel hostage. U.S. president Jimmy Carter pressured Iran to release the hostages. But months went by with no progress in negotiations. In the meantime, military authorities began planning a daring assault that would free the hostages. On April 11, 1980, President Carter approved the mission, code-named Operation Eagle Claw.

Unfortunately, the operation proved to be a fiasco. Communication among the different armed forces units broke down, equipment failed, and eight American servicemen died. Photos of the smoking wreckage of American aircraft circulated throughout the world. As the men who had planned the operation cataloged the factors that led to its failure, one thing became obvious. The Marine pilots of the helicopters that flew from an American aircraft carrier to carry out vital segments of the operation lacked the necessary training and experience. Nighttime flying at low altitudes while being buffeted by high winds laden with sand was unlike anything they had ever done. It wasn't just the Marines, either. No helicopter unit in the entire U.S. military had the background and ability to carry out this kind of mission.

With the hostages still in captivity, military officials decided to try again. Planning began for Operation Honey Badger, which would tap into the expertise of the army's 101st Airborne Division (Air Assault). Organizers also took advantage of a new helicopter, the UH-60 Black Hawk. Volunteer pilots from the 101st began to undertake seemingly endless hours of nighttime flying. One of the key skills they needed to master was nap-of-the-earth (NOE), or extremely low-altitude flying. They learned to use Earth's terrain to their advantage. For example, they might fly in the gap between two hills, rather than over them, to avoid de-

The former U.S. embassy in Iran is now used as a staging ground for anti-American demonstrations.

> **FORCE FACTS** Without simulator training in aerial refueling, it often takes pilots a dozen tries to make the first "plug" in real-life practice. With this training, pilots usually make the hookup on their first or second try.

tection. Sometimes they even flew under power lines and had to pull up sharply to avoid road signs. NOE is dangerous enough during daylight hours, but new night-vision technology helped make this type of flying possible. By the fall of 1980, the pilots were deemed combat-ready. However, the hostages were released the day Ronald Reagan became president in 1981, scrubbing the operation.

The army felt the experience the pilots had gained was too valuable to waste, though. It reorganized the unit into the 160th Aviation Battalion on October 16, 1981. Veterans of the original battalion refer to that date as "the day the Eagles came off." That referenced the division's longstanding nickname, the "Screaming Eagles," as well as the *iconic* emblem on the shoulder patches of members of the 101st Airborne. The battalion's new patches depicted a sword-swinging grim reaper riding a winged horse. "Death Waits in the Dark" was embroidered above the image, with "Night Stalkers" underneath. Eventually, the unit's name was changed to the 160th Special Operations Aviation Regiment (Airborne).

The men continued their rigorous training. They participated in Operation Urgent Fury, the attack on the Caribbean island of Grenada in 1983. A communist-leaning organization had overthrown the island's governor general. The Reagan administration felt the new regime could pose a threat to the U.S. During the operation, the Night Stalkers had three primary tasks that involved carrying troops to key locations to attack enemy head-

Refueling helicopters in the air saves time and helps the aircraft avoid detection in having to land.

quarters, rescue the governor-general, and secure an important radio transmitter. Despite the challenges, the Night Stalkers successfully carried out their assigned missions.

SOAR (A)'s first night operation came in 1987. Iranian ships were laying mines in an area of the Persian Gulf where loaded oil tankers regularly passed. The deadly mines threatened the transportation of oil. Special Forces were dispatched to the region in what became known as Operation Earnest Will and Operation Prime Chance. Soon after the operations began, Night Stalkers fired on the vessel *Iran Ajr*, which carried dozens of mines. A Navy SEAL team boarded the badly damaged vessel and *scuttled* it. The Night Stalkers remained on a floating station in the gulf for more than a year.

Two years later, Night Stalkers played a key role in Operation Just Cause. The goals of this mission were the liberation of Panama and the arrest of its dictator, General Manuel Noriega. Demand for Night Stalker services increased substantially during Operation Desert Storm, which began in 1991 after Iraqi dictator Saddam Hussein invaded neighboring Kuwait. It was the

Night Stalker pilots are capable of flying over all types of terrain at any time of day to reach their target on time.

first time that the entire regiment was in action at the same time. Night Stalkers were especially important in helping to locate and destroy dozens of Scud missiles. Hussein had planned on launching the missiles into Israel to provoke them into fighting. That would have upset the delicate balance among U.S. and Arab *coalition* forces. The Arabs would almost certainly have balked at fighting on the same side as Israel. The two sides have been in conflict for decades, and it is likely that neither would be willing to come to the other's defense. Night Stalkers also ferried numerous *reconnaissance* teams behind Iraqi lines.

The Night Stalkers nearly had the opportunity to redeem the failure of Operation Eagle Claw. Hussein's forces had taken a number of hostages in the early stages of the invasion. Hussein threatened to use those hostages as human shields and refused to negotiate their release. Night Stalkers and Delta Force operators painstakingly rehearsed a mission to free the hostages. All personnel involved felt confident of success. But Hussein eventually decided to release the hostages.

In 1993, Night Stalkers were involved in an operation in civil-war-torn Somalia. Their mission was to seize several high-ranking warlords. What was planned as a quick *insertion* and *extraction* turned into a deadly firefight. Two Black Hawk helicopters were shot down. Five crewmen were among the 19 Americans killed. The aircraft flown by the Night Stalkers gave the name to author Mark Bowden's book *Black Hawk Down* and its film adaptation.

Since the U.S. response to the 9/11 terror attacks, Night Stalker operations in the Middle East have remained continual. No matter the obstacles or the mission, the unit continues to perform at the highest level.

Known for their heavy-lifting capacity, military versions of the Chinook have grown more powerful over the years.

FORCE FACTS Ongoing retrofits to the Chinook may extend its operational life into the 2060s, when many of the aircraft will be almost 100 years old.

BIRDS OF PREY

To fulfill its missions, Night Stalkers employ three distinct helicopters. From the earliest days of the unit, its members have worked closely with manufacturers to ensure that every new variation increases their capability to carry out missions. The smallest helicopter is the AH/MH-6 Little Bird. It is one of the most maneuverable and agile military helicopters in the world. At 32 feet (10 m) long, it has a cruising speed of about 155 miles (250 km) per hour and a range of 230 miles (370 km). The Little Bird can land on city streets, bridges, and rooftops. Experienced pilots can even touch down briefly on surfaces as narrow as concrete traffic barriers while maintaining complete control of the aircraft.

While the Little Bird requires only one pilot, it's customary to have two seated in its distinctively bubble-shaped glass cockpit. They are the only crew members. The Little Bird has two variants. The unarmed MH version is designed to insert troops. It carries as many as six people, three on each side of the open compartment immediately behind the pilots. It takes a special breed of soldier to sit on a plank mounted on a Little Bird, feet dangling in the air or resting on the skids, surrounded by darkness and buffeted by the wind the aircraft makes as it powers forward. The MH-6 can also be fitted with racks capable of carrying two motorcycles.

The AH-6 is a light attack helicopter. It packs weapons such as the M134 mini-gun—a 6-barrel Gatling gun capable of blast-

The Little Bird can be broken down for transport on cargo planes and then quickly reassembled at its destination.

FORCE FACTS In addition to their service in the U.S. military, Chinooks are a valued part of the military forces of 18 other countries around the world.

ing up to 6,000 rounds per minute, pods holding up to a dozen rockets, Hellfire laser-guided anti-tank missiles, grenade launchers, .50-caliber machine guns, and even air-to-air Stinger missiles.

To get where they are needed, Little Birds are loaded onto transport aircraft. The C-130 Hercules, for example, can carry up to three Little Birds. The helicopters can be mission-ready within as little as 15 minutes after the Hercules touches down.

The second Night Stalker helicopter is the MH-60 Black Hawk, one of the most famous U.S. military aircraft. It is 50 feet (15 m) long, cruises at 160 miles (260 km) per hour, and has a *combat radius* slightly larger than 300 miles (480 km). The four-man crew consists of a pilot, copilot, and two crew chiefs/door gunners who fire M134s from each side of the aircraft. It can accommodate a complete 12-person Operational Detachment–Alpha (ODA) and all their equipment. Black Hawks can also be used for resupply, search and rescue, and evacuation of wounded soldiers.

A variant of the Black Hawk is the Direct Action Penetrator (DAP) gunship, which is fitted with Lightweight Armament Support Structure (LASS). This includes a reinforced stub wing on either side of the aircraft, which can mount a variety of weapons systems to vastly increase the Black Hawk's firepower. In addition to mini-guns, it can carry M230 30-mm *chain guns*; up to four 2.75-inch, 19-tube rocket pods; as many as 16 AGM-114 Hellfire missiles; air-to-air Stinger missiles; and a .50-caliber, 3-barrel Gatling gun.

Like their smaller cousins, Black Hawks fit into larger air force transport planes. The C-5 Galaxy, for example, can carry up to six. It takes about an hour to prepare and load the helicopters onto the aircraft and another hour after landing to make them flight-ready.

The third helicopter—and by far the largest—is the MH-47G Chinook. With its two 60-foot- diameter (18 m) rotors, it is among the most distinctive aircraft in the U.S. military. It is more than 50

Among the world's largest military aircraft, the C-5 Galaxy has been in operation since 1970.

FORCE FACTS An ODA is usually led by a captain, with a warrant officer as second-in-command. The remaining 10 operators are sergeants, and all have individual specialties.

feet (15 m) long and more than 12 feet (4 m) wide. It can soar to 20,000 feet (6,000 m). At a cruising speed of just under 185 miles (300 km) per hour, the Chinook has a mission radius of more than 200 miles (320 km). Midair refueling significantly increases that range. In addition to a crew of 5—pilot, copilot, flight engineer, and 2 crew chiefs—it can carry up to 55 more people or several tons of cargo. The Chinook is armed with a pair of M134 miniguns, one on each side by the forward doors. It may also mount M240D machine guns on the ramp. Despite its size, a Chinook fits in a C-5 Galaxy to be transported to wherever it is needed.

Regardless of their size, all three birds have one job in common: getting boots on the ground on time and on target. Besides landing on the ground, there are several methods of inserting troops. The primary one is fast-roping. A crew member throws a thick rope out of the aircraft. Even before it hits the ground, the soldiers are sliding down. They wear heavy gloves to protect their hands from the heat and friction generated by the swift descent. An entire ODA team can be on the ground in less than 15 seconds. A caving ladder allows them to quickly climb back aboard the helicopter when the mission is over. An electronically operated hoist mounted above the doorway provides another way for soldiers to return to the helicopter.

Both of these extraction methods can be time-consuming. When the men have to *exfiltrate* immediately, the hovering helicopter will drop a rope with numerous rings. Each operator—as Special Forces troops are often called—wears a special harness that clips onto one of the rings. The harness allows at least one hand to be free so the men can fire at pursuers. As soon as everyone is secured to the rope, the aircraft lifts off with the men dangling below and flies to a secure location.

While Black Hawks hover to drop off or pick up troops, the helicopter's gunner can lay down cover fire.

Though the Chinook looks awkward and ungainly, the skilled pilots of the 160th can perform an amazing array of maneuvers to get their operators to their destinations and safely home. One is the "Rubber Duck" insertion. While the pilot hovers a few feet above a body of water, crew members push a Zodiac rubber raft out of the rear ramp. Moments later, the team leaps into the water, swims to the Zodiac, clambers aboard, fires up the engine, and is on its way. The "Delta Queen" is the reverse of the Rubber Duck. It is employed when the team needs a fast exfiltration. As the Zodiac speeds toward the helicopter, the pilot lowers the ramp and descends until the chopper rests on the surface. Water floods into the fuselage, a foot (0.3 m) deep or even more. The Zodiac driver aims the boat toward the ramp, guns the engine, and zooms up the ramp. The team scrambles out and helps the crew pull the watercraft farther forward. The

Chinooks can also move watercraft via hoist cables: crewmen rig the boat to the helicopter before climbing a rope ladder.

ramp begins to close behind them. The pilot immediately lifts upward and tilts the rear slightly downward. This allows water to drain out. The whole process takes only a few seconds.

In terms of overall organization, SOAR (A) is part of the U.S. Special Operations Command (SOCOM). The regiment has four battalions. Each has three to five helicopter companies as well as headquarters and maintenance companies. The regimental headquarters company and training facilities are located at the sprawling Fort Campbell, which straddles the western portion of the Kentucky–Tennessee border. Fort Campbell is also home to the unit's First Battalion. It consists of the following:

- Light Assault Company Alpha—15 MH-6 Little Birds
- Light Attack Reconnaissance Company Bravo—15 AH-6 Little Birds
- Assault Company Charlie—10 MH-60 Black Hawks
- Assault Company Delta—10 MH-60 Black Hawks
- Assault Company Echo—10 MH-60 DAP Black Hawks

Second Battalion is also based at Fort Campbell. It is configured as follows:

- Heavy Helicopter Company Alpha—8 MH-47G Chinooks
- Heavy Helicopter Company Bravo—8 MH-47G Chinooks
- Assault Company Charlie—10 MH-60 Black Hawks

Third Battalion is headquartered at Hunter Army Airfield in Savannah, Georgia. Fourth Battalion is located at Joint Base Lewis–McChord near Tacoma, Washington. Both of these battalions have the same configuration as Second Battalion.

Night Stalkers train for insertions and extractions on land as well as over water.

FORCE FACTS A system called Helicopter Alert and Threat Termination-Acoustic (HALTT-A) is capable of detecting the sound of an enemy's round leaving a weapon and fixing the shooter's position so that he can be "terminated."

LEARNING HOW TO DELIVER

IT TAKES EXCEPTIONAL INDIVIDUALS TO COMPLETE DEMANDing missions under especially stressful conditions. Night Stalker candidates undergo intense training that pushes them to their physical and mental limits. In the unit's early days, there was considerable pressure to learn and do as much as possible in a minimal amount of time. Sometimes that meant bending—or even breaking—established regulations. A series of accidents in 1983 cost the lives of 16 men. A panel of experienced aviators conducted a detailed study of the causes of the accidents.

As a result of the inquiry, a highly structured training program, known as Green Platoon, was established. Training takes place at Fort Campbell and is run by the Special Operations Aviation Training Company (SOATC). The instructors are former SOAR (A) members with years of hands-on experience. All candidates are volunteers. A few exceptional students come to Green Platoon directly from flight school. The majority are experienced pilots with thousands of hours' worth of flight time.

The process begins with a weeklong assessment. This includes examination of military records, interviews, psychological evaluations, and two flights. During this time, instructors try to determine candidates' motivation and their ability to be trained. "It's not necessarily that we are better aviators," said a longtime pilot. "We are much more motivated than the average aviator. Our attitudes are completely different.... Everything in the regiment is trained to exceed any possible *parameter* of failure." At the end of the week, candidates find out whether they have been

Candidates entering Night Stalkers training start out learning skills in combat, weaponry, and survival.

FORCE FACTS Several AH-6 Little Birds gained a measure of revenge for the 1993 disaster in Mogadishu 16 years later when they returned to Somalia and helped to kill terrorist leader Saleh Ali Saleh Nabhan.

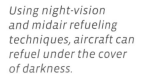
admitted to Green Platoon.

Once accepted, *enlisted* personnel spend five to six weeks learning skills such as hand-to-hand combat, firing a variety of weapons, and combat first aid. They perform demanding field exercises before moving on to more technical courses. Pilots also undergo survival, evasion, resistance, and escape (SERE) training. After that, they begin rigorous flight training. Up first is a month-long training in aerial navigation in Little Birds. Then the pilots transition to a four-month advanced skills course. This focuses on the specific type of helicopter they will fly. They spend many hours in simulator training. They also fly in a variety of conditions and terrain, with special emphasis on conducting *infiltration* and exfiltration missions.

Unlike most other Special Forces training courses, which have high washout rates, few prospective Night Stalkers fail to complete the course. Trainers credit this high success rate to the motivation of the pilots and the thoroughness of the assessment phase. At the end of training, pilots become basic mission qualified (BMQ) and join their assigned battalion. They serve as copilots with more experienced pilots during operational missions. After serving with their unit for at least a year and a half, they become fully mission-qualified (FMQ). This enables them to command an aircraft during an operational mission. After another three or four years, they become flight lead qualified (FLQ), which involves planning and leading individual missions.

Despite the swashbuckling reputation of Night Stalkers, there are surprisingly few depictions of this group in popular culture. "Their entire mission is to not be seen, not be noticed," says author M. L. Buchman. "If you go to your local big bookstore or major library, you will find whole shelves on SEALs and Delta Force, though much of the latter has little to do with what I can discover of the reality. If you find even one book about the Night

Using night-vision and midair refueling techniques, aircraft can refuel under the cover of darkness.

FORCE FACTS Besides writing the Night Stalkers series and dozens of other novels, M. L. Buchman has ridden his bike around the world, rebuilt a 50-foot (15 m) sailboat, flown and jumped out of airplanes, and designed and built two houses.

Stalkers in either place, it will be unusual."

Buchman has written more than a dozen Night Stalkers romantic suspense novels. The series began in 2012 with *The Night Is Mine*. The novel proved to be somewhat **prescient**, as the heroine, Captain Emily Beale, becomes the first woman to pilot a Night Stalker Black Hawk. In real life, that didn't happen until 2013. Many readers praise the book's military realism, technical terminology, and extended mission descriptions. In naming the series' second book as one of the best romances of 2012, Eloisa James of National Public Radio (NPR) noted, "[Buchman's] Night Stalkers series turns a passion for military helicopters into a fundamental characteristic of his heroines. These women are the ultimate alpha soldiers—although it should be said that the novels do not glorify the American military. What they do glorify is a military chopper with four seats—'the nastiest gunship God ever put on Earth and only the best flew in her,' as the heroine of *I Own the Dawn,* Sergeant Kee Smith, puts it."

Night Stalkers are probably best known because of Mark Bowden's gripping account of the failed 1993 Somalia operation. *Black Hawk Down: A Story of Modern War* was published in 1999. It became a finalist for that year's National Book Award in the nonfiction category. An accompanying video aired a month after the book's publishing date and won an Emmy. Critics and readers alike praised the book for its gritty realism and inclusion of the underlying political and economic factors that led to the infamous battle.

Two years later, the book was made into a film. *Black Hawk Down* topped the box office during the first three weeks of its nationwide release. The movie won Oscars for film editing and sound mixing. For the most part, critics liked it. *Empire* magazine termed it "a rare find of a war movie which dares to turn **genre** convention on its head." Evan Thomas of *Newsweek* said,

After six months of training, pilots serve with an operational unit for at least two years before they are fully mission-qualified.

"Though it depicted a shameful defeat, the soldiers were heroes willing to die for their brothers in arms. The movie showed brutal scenes of killing, but also courage, *stoicism*, and honor. The overall effect was stirring, ... and it seemed to enhance the desire of Americans for a thumping war to avenge 9/11 [which had occurred only a few months earlier, though the filming had been completed months before that]." It also received high marks from Rotten Tomatoes. The film rating website noted, "Though it's light on character development and cultural empathy, *Black Hawk Down* is a visceral, pulse-pounding portrait of war, elevated by [director] Ridley Scott's superb technical skill."

Another audience had a very different reaction when an illegally copied version was shown in Somalia. Many attendees had participated in the real-life event. Not surprisingly, they leaped up in glee when helicopters crashed or Americans were shot. On a more serious note, one man said, "I lost nine of my best friends in one spot. It was that very helicopter. It hovered on top of us, and shot us, one by one. I got wounded, but the others died." Other Somalis worried about the way Americans would perceive them after watching the film. "There is not a single word of the Somali language, no Somali music, nothing of our culture," one man complained. "The Somali people are depicted as very savage beasts without any human element," said another. He added that the movie was a setback to efforts by American Somalis to show that they overwhelmingly supported the U.S. in the War on Terror.

The book was also adapted for a first-person-shooter video game called *Delta Force: Black Hawk Down*. Developed by Nova-Logic, it was released for Microsoft Windows in 2003, for Mac OS X in 2004, and for both PlayStation 2 and Xbox the following year. *Maxim* gave it an 8/10 rating, noting, "While it would be impossible for the game to mimic the raw emotion and chaos that defined this mission-turned-disaster in real life, the graphics are the best we've seen on a battlefield."

Black Hawk Down *dramatized the events of the failed 1993 Battle of Mogadishu mission in Somalia.*

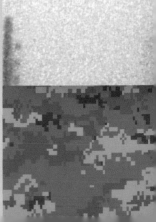

FORCE FACTS In 2004, Black Hawk helicopters played a key role in carrying Delta Force operators to free four hostages in Iraq.

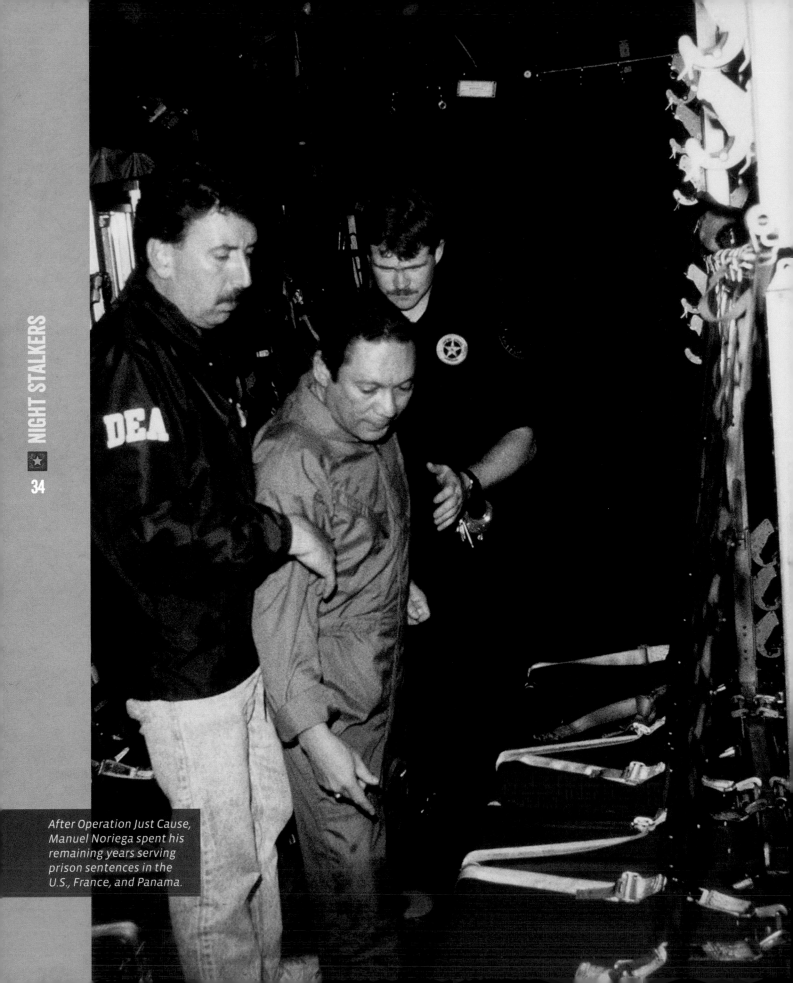

After Operation Just Cause, Manuel Noriega spent his remaining years serving prison sentences in the U.S., France, and Panama.

NOTABLE MISSIONS

U.S. SPECIAL FORCES

THE FIRST MAJOR NIGHT STALKER MISSION WAS OPERATION Just Cause, the invasion of Panama in December 1989. It involved a number of pre-assault missions. SOAR (A) inserted Air Force combat controllers into a major airfield. There the controllers set out beacons for a paratroop assault. The Night Stalkers delivered Army Rangers to seize another airfield. They used MH-6s to fly Delta Force operators to a prison to liberate a U.S. citizen named Kurt Muse. Meanwhile, Little Bird gunships provided air cover. Their final task involved helping to find the hiding place of Panamanian dictator Manuel Noriega (which they called the "hunt for Elvis [Presley]").

After finding Noriega, they flew him to a nearby airfield. He was loaded onto an Air Force transport helicopter and taken to Florida. The only downside to the operation came during a raid on a house containing several of Noriega's top aides. One Little Bird was shot down, killing the pilots. They were the only Night Stalkers to die in the operation.

One of the Night Stalkers' most famous missions took place in Mogadishu, Somalia. A civil war among powerful warlords and the country's weak central government had created a humanitarian crisis. Supported by the United Nations, convoys sought to deliver food and other supplies to the people. The warlords repeatedly attacked the convoys. The U.S. responded with Operation Restore Hope in late 1992. Thousands of troops were sent to the country to secure routes for the humanitarian convoys. On

Since 9/11, the Night Stalkers have remained on active duty, but they strive to go unnoticed.

FORCE FACTS Besides the U.S. Army, the only other organization that uses the Little Bird is the FBI's Hostage Rescue Team.

October 3, 1993, a group of Rangers and Delta Force operators was tasked with capturing two of the warlords. According to the plan for what was called Operation Gothic Serpent, two Little Birds would take Delta Force to the target building. At the same time, dozens of Rangers would fast-rope down from hovering Black Hawks to provide a defensive perimeter. A ground force would swoop in and ferry the operators and prisoners back to base. The whole operation would take about 30 minutes.

German general Helmuth von Moltke is famous for saying, "No plan survives contact with the enemy." This certainly proved to be true with Operation Gothic Serpent. The snatch-and-grab portion worked perfectly. Nothing else did. Things started unraveling when a Ranger fell about 70 feet (21 m) from one of the Black Hawks. He required immediate evacuation, but by this time, hundreds—perhaps thousands—of armed Somali militiamen had converged on the site. Soon after, one of the Black Hawks was shot down, killing the pilot and copilot and injuring the crewmen. Another Black Hawk went down a few minutes later. No one was killed in the second crash, but hundreds of Somalis swarmed to the crash site. Heroic resistance from Delta Force snipers Gary Gordon and Randy Shughart briefly kept the enemy away from the wreckage, but the two men—both later awarded the Medal of Honor—ran out of ammunition. The Somalis killed everyone in the wreckage except the pilot, Michael Durant. They took him prisoner.

The Rangers and Delta Force were still cut off. As night fell, the Somalis launched repeated attacks. But intense fire from the trapped American forces, combined with *strafing* and rocket attacks from Little Bird gunships, kept them from being overrun. A relief column finally got through the following day and conveyed the men to safety. Durant was released after 11 days. Analysis later indicated that the operation had experienced the highest intensity and volume of fire since the Vietnam War.

The Night Stalkers and other special forces have learned from the mistakes of past missions.

FORCE FACTS The "screaming eagle" emblem of the 101st Airborne Division dates back to its 1921 formation in Wisconsin. It honors "Old Abe," an eagle that was the mascot of a Wisconsin volunteer regiment in the Civil War.

One of the best-known—and most tragic—Night Stalker missions occurred in Afghanistan in late June 2005. Operation Red Wings was tasked with disrupting enemy activity in the harsh terrain of Kunar Province, thereby creating a stable environment for elections scheduled that September. The plan was to insert a four-man SEAL team into the rugged mountains to conduct reconnaissance and surveillance. A Marine battalion would then use this information to attack. Like Operation Gothic Serpent, Red Wings got off to a good start. A Chinook inserted the SEALs, who quickly moved into a concealed position. But also like Gothic Serpent, the operation then fell apart. The position wasn't concealed enough. Local goat herders discovered the SEALs and betrayed them to *insurgents*, who swarmed them with assault rifles, machine guns, and heavier weapons. The SEALs sent a desperate message about their plight. The Night Stalkers didn't hesitate to mount a quick rescue plan, even though it was broad daylight.

Recognizing the urgency of the situation, two Chinooks raced ahead of heavily armed Apache helicopters that could have laid down suppressing fire. Stripped of the concealment of night, the Chinooks were dangerously vulnerable. In addition, there was only one place to land. All the enemy had to do was lie in wait. As the Chinooks began their descent, an insurgent rose to his feet and fired a rocket-propelled grenade. The projectile slammed into one of the helicopters. "The aircraft nearly inverted and then came apart, and it exploded prior to hitting the ground," said the pilot of the other helicopter. "No one ever survives them before they hit the ground." All 16 men on board—8 SEALs and 8 Night Stalkers—perished. So did three of the men they had tried to rescue. The fourth was rescued by friendly Afghans.

Pilots involved in Operation Honey Badger were from the 101st Airborne Division, nicknamed the "Screaming Eagles."

Storm clouds developed, and the remaining helicopters had to return to base. The bodies of the fallen men were recovered several days later. In the close-knit ranks of the Night Stalkers, the pain was almost unbearable. As they unloaded the body bags from the recovery helicopter, one man said, "That was the worst day of my life, and one that I relive on a constant basis. It's with me always."

Navy SEAL Team Six received widespread acclaim for taking advantage of an intelligence breakthrough that pinpointed the location of Osama bin Laden. The team launched a successful attack on May 2, 2011. It's no surprise that the Night Stalkers delivered the men to bin Laden's walled compound in Pakistan. The assault team flew to its destination on two specially modified Black Hawks. In addition, two Chinooks, carrying 24 SEALs, were on standby on the ground elsewhere in Pakistan, ready to intervene if needed. Two more Chinooks remained in Afghanistan,

The Night Stalkers have successfully delivered soldiers and saved lives in many important operations.

ready with still more SEAL reinforcements.

The Black Hawks lifted off before midnight. They remained undetected during the 90-minute flight to the target. According to plan, one aircraft would hover above the interior of the court-yard as the SEALs fast-roped down and forced their way into the house. The other helicopter would remain just outside the walls while the men it carried secured the perimeter.

But the Black Hawk hovering inside the compound encoun-tered a problem. The combination of higher-than-expected tem-peratures and the height of the walls kept the rotor *downwash* from properly diffusing. The aircraft began descending. The tail assembly brushed against a wall, threatening a loss of control. Drawing on his years of experience, the pilot quickly buried the nose of the aircraft into the ground. The "soft landing" kept the helicopter from flipping over and seriously injuring or even kill-ing the men inside. When bin Laden had been killed and the oper-ation completed, the men set explosive charges on the damaged helicopter because it was not flyable. One of the standby Chi-nooks and the second Black Hawk flew the men and bin Laden's body out of Pakistan.

Former chairman of the Joint Chiefs of Staff General Henry Shelton summed up the feelings of countless American service-men and women about the Night Stalkers. "Throughout the short history of the 160th," he said, "its aviators have pioneered night flight tactics and techniques, led the development of new equip-ment and procedures, met the call to duty wherever it sounded, and earned a reputation for excellence and valor that is second to none." The world remains a dangerous place, but there is no doubt that the Night Stalkers will continue living up to Shelton's words. The "FedEx" of Special Forces will make its "deliveries" on time, every time.

Those who don't become Night Stalker pilots train to be flight engineers and gunners.

FORCE FACTS In 1988, two Night Stalker Chinooks extracted an abandoned Soviet Mi-24 attack helicopter from North Africa so that it could be brought to the U.S. and examined.

More than 3,000 personnel make up the elite Night Stalkers regiment today.

FORCE FACTS Fort Campbell is named for General William Bowen Campbell, who served in the Mexican-American War and later was governor of Tennessee.

GLOSSARY

chain guns – weapons driven by a continuous loop of chain similar to a bicycle

coalition – a temporary alliance to undertake a combined action

combat radius – the distance a military aircraft can fly to a designated site, remain for a set period of time, and return

downwash – downward air turbulence caused by a helicopter rotor

enlisted – describing those who sign up voluntarily or are drafted for military duty at a rank below an officer; they compose the largest part of military units

exfiltrate – to remove personnel from enemy-controlled territory by means of stealth

extraction – the safe withdrawal from a mission

genre – a category of artistic or other type of composition having many qualities in common

iconic – something that is very famous and represents a particular thing or idea

infiltration – secretive passage into enemy-held territory

insertion – the secret placing of troops in an enemy-held area

insurgents – rebels; those in armed resistance to a government

parameter – a measureable factor

prescient – accurately foretelling the future

reconnaissance – a search to gain information, usually conducted in secret

scuttled – deliberately sank

stoicism – uncomplaining acceptance of hardship or pain

strafing – attacking from low-flying aircraft, most commonly with machine guns

Taliban – a fundamentalist Islamic political movement and militia in Afghanistan; noted especially for terror tactics and a repressive attitude toward women

FORCE FACTS Delta Queen extractions in salt water have a downside. Because salt is corrosive, engines and exposed machinery need a thorough cleaning after each extraction.

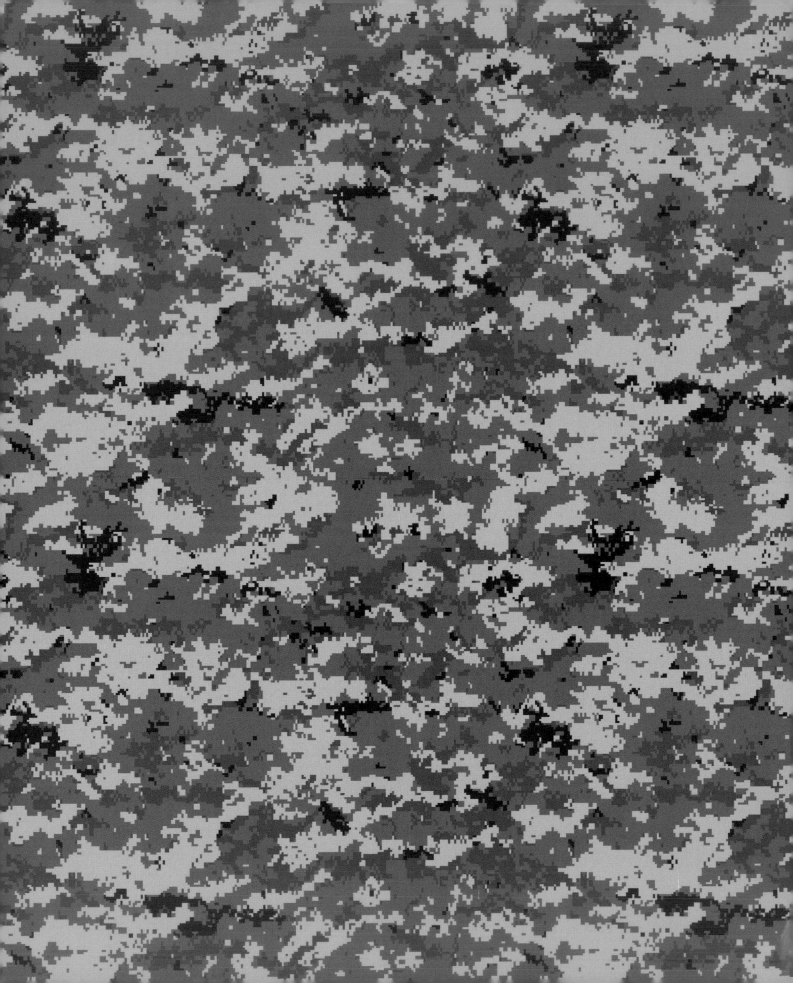

SELECTED BIBLIOGRAPHY

U.S. SPECIAL FORCES

Bowden, Mark. *Black Hawk Down: A Story of Modern War.* New York: Grove Press, 2010.

Crosby, Francis. *The World Encyclopedia of Military Helicopters.* London: Lorenz Books, 2013.

Durant, Michael J., and Steven Hartov. *The Night Stalkers: Top Secret Missions of the U.S. Army's Special Operations Aviation Regiment.* With Lt. Col. Robert L. Johnson. New York: New American Library, 2008.

Frederick, Jim. *Special Ops: The Hidden World of America's Toughest Warriors.* New York: Time Books, 2011.

Luttrell, Marcus. *Lone Survivor: The Eyewitness Account of Operation Redwing and the Lost Heroes of SEAL Team 10.* With Patrick Robinson. New York: Little, Brown, 2007.

Neville, Leigh. *Special Forces in the War on Terror.* Oxford, UK: Osprey, 2015.

Pushies, Fred J. *Night Stalkers: 160th Special Operations Aviation Regiment (Airborne).* St. Paul, Minn.: Zenith Press, 2005.

Stanton, Doug. *Horse Soldiers: The Extraordinary Story of a Band of U.S. Soldiers Who Rode to Victory in Afghanistan.* New York: Scribner, 2009.

WEBSITES

160th Doing Delta Queen Maneuver

https://www.bing.com/videos/search?q=delta+queen+chinook+&&view=detail&mid=F1EE2158361AB9DB4BF0F1EE2158361AB9DB4BF0&FORM=VRDGAR

Chinook Picks up Navy SEALs from the Water

https://www.bing.com/videos/search?q=delta+queen+chinook+&&view=detail&mid=CE26EC9679EE4C4E9E4BCE26EC9679EE4C4E9E4B&FORM=VRDGAR

These two videos show members of the 160th doing the Delta Queen maneuver.

160th Special Operations Aviation Regiment—Night Stalkers—160th SOAR

https://www.bing.com/videos/search?q=160th+SOAR+helicopters&&view=detail&mid=D20973F2DB617C04C960D20973F2DB617C04C960&FORM=VRDGAR

This video features extensive footage of all three Night Stalkers helicopters in a combination of actual missions and training exercises.

READ MORE

Brush, Jim. *Special Forces.* Mankato, Minn.: Sea-to-Sea, 2012.

Cooper, Jason. *U.S. Special Operations.* Vero Beach, Fla.: Rourke, 2004.

INDEX